Colour
me
Mindful

Also in the series:

Colour
me
Mindful

UNDERWATER

Anastasia Catris

Copyright © Orion 2015

The right of Orion to be identified as the author
of this work has been asserted in accordance with
the Copyright, Designs and Patents Act 1988.

This edition first published in Great Britain in 2015
by Orion
an imprint of the Orion Publishing Group Ltd
Carmelite House
50 Victoria Embankment
London EC4Y 0DZ
An Hachette UK Company

3 5 7 9 10 8 6 4 2

A CIP catalogue record for this book
is available from the British Library.

ISBN: 978 1 4091 6306 0

Printed in Italy

The Orion Publishing Group's policy is to use papers
that are natural, renewable and recyclable and made
from wood grown in sustainable forests. The logging and
manufacturing processes are expected to conform to the
environmental regulations of the country of origin.

Every effort has been made to fulfil requirements with regard
to reproducing copyright material. The author and publisher will
be glad to rectify any omissions at the earliest opportunity.

www.orionbooks.co.uk

Introduction

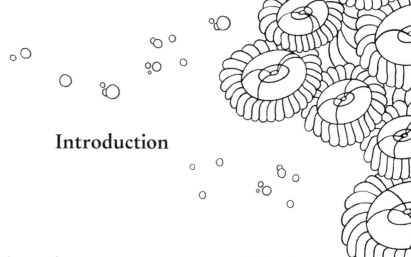

Mindfulness is the art of present moment awareness, of being alert and relaxed at once. Art is a wonderful gateway to this state. As you colour with focus and attention, your stress will start to fade. As you watch closely to stay within the lines, your worries will seem to lessen. And as you lose yourself in the wonders of colour and creativity, your surroundings will come alive and seem a little brighter.

It's a busy world we live in and you might sometimes feel as if life is rushing by, one thing after another. For many, this rushing is code for that thing we call stress, that constant striving to find happiness through one more success, through one more experience, leading to a feeling of exhaustion and a massive to-do list!

If your world feels like this, it's time to slow down. So put down your tasks, your goals and your worries, just for a moment (or maybe an hour). Allow yourself to recharge by taking a little holiday from thinking, stepping into the present moment and colouring in the beautiful shapes and patterns in this book.

Take a breath and feel the air coming and going. Pick up a crayon and begin to gradually fill this world with colour. Let this moment be as it is. Learning to focus and enjoy simple things like colouring once more can lead to the happiness everyone deserves.

Oli Doyle
Author of *Mindfulness Plain & Simple* and *Mindfulness for Life*
www.peacethroughmindfulness.com.au

About the author

After graduating from Royal Holloway, University of London with a BA Hons in English Literature, Anastasia Catris travelled to the United States to pursue her passion for illustration by studying at The Kubert School of Comic and Cartoon Art.

She returned to the UK in 2009, and has since worked as a freelance illustrator for HarperCollins, *Kerrang!*, Fox, Marvel, DC and *Cygnus Alpha: The Doctor Who Fanzine*. Ana lives in Wales, United Kingdom, and is an advocate of art therapy and of the calming power of colouring in.

www.anastasiacatris.com
Instagram: @AnastasiaCatris

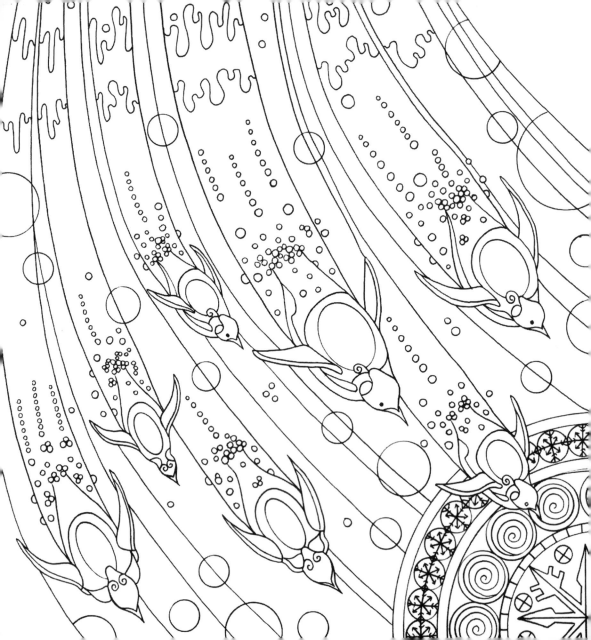

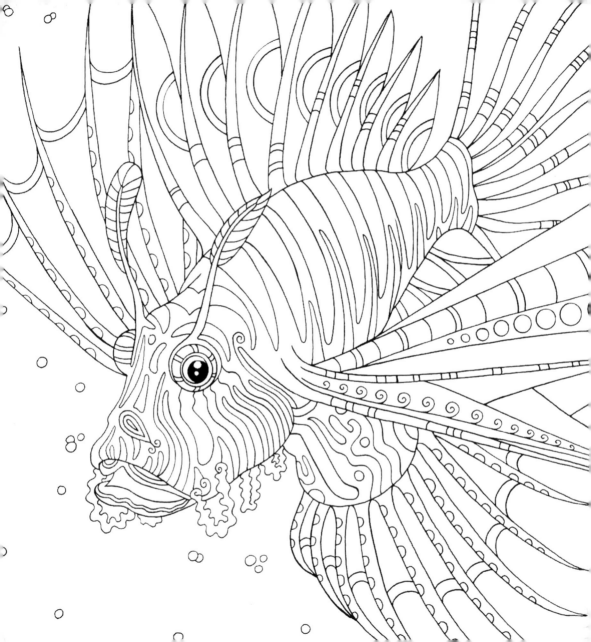

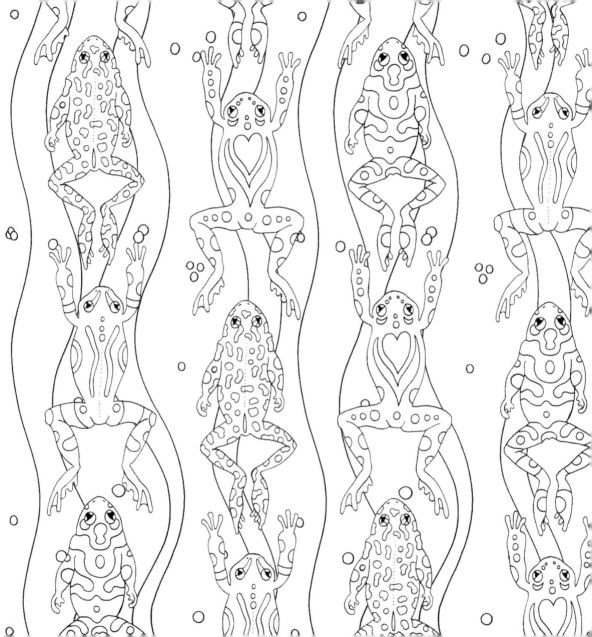

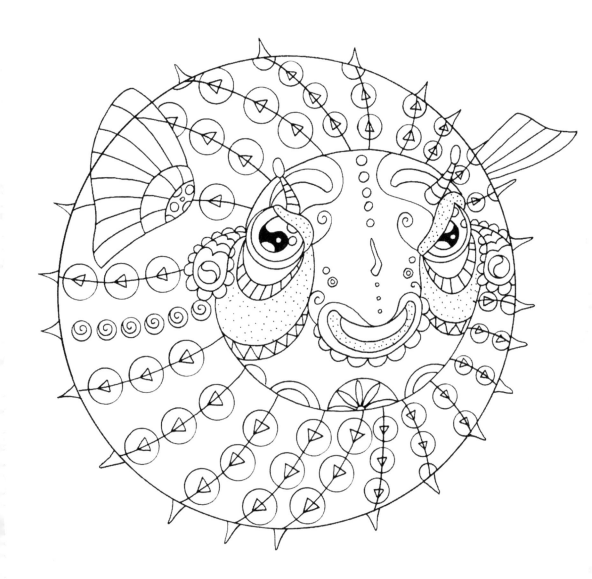

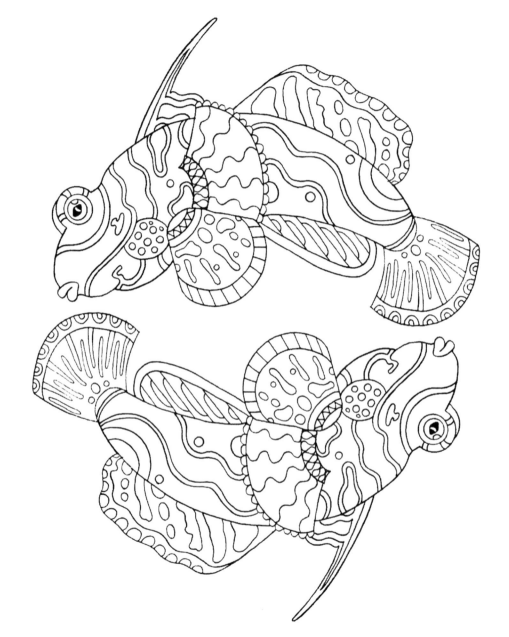

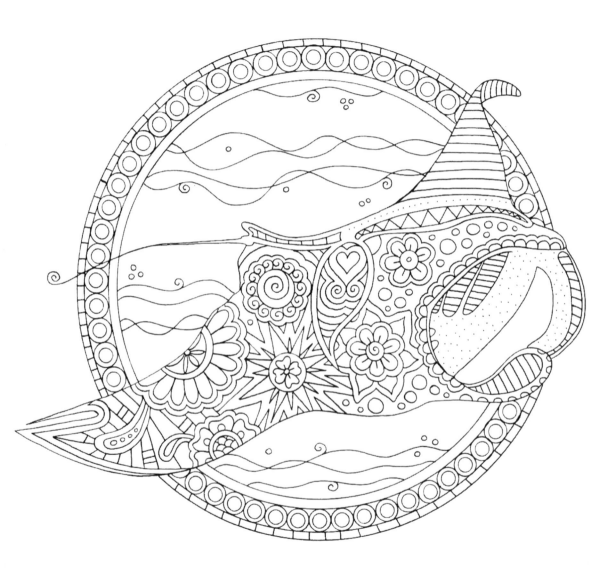

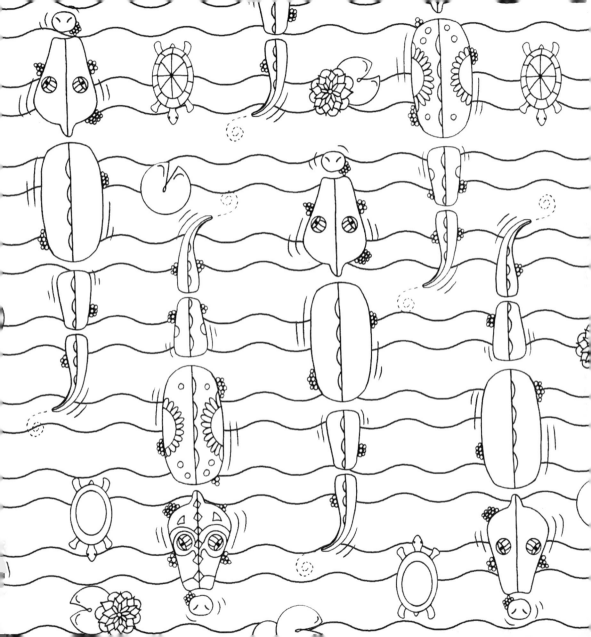

Collect all the books in the

Colour
me
Mindful

series

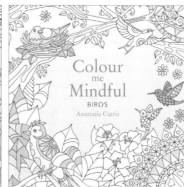

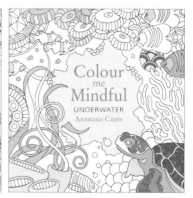